The Nest

Giordana Chirissi

Illustrated by Lilia Batel

for Mimi

The green-eyed cat called Odin has always felt vastly superior to everyone around him. He is vain, bold and not very fond of humans. However, if truth be told, there is one notable exception. Her name is Anna, and he thinks she is a sensational seamstress: original, diligent, witty, – and, most importantly – she means what she says.

It has always been a great pleasure to visit her windowsill overlooking the garden. Odin shares the spot with a lush geranium that often turns into a useful tool of disguise. He shows his affection for Anna by gently clawing at her arm, and she always returns the kindness. Tenderness is a serious thing!

Time and again, Odin comes around for a tasty treat, but mostly because he feels welcome. He has humorously named Anna's place the House of Thousand Spools, since spools are everywhere there. He has seen them in flowerpots, cookie jars and some really odd places.

For instance, the garden's finch, known as Fin "of the long twittering song", enjoys toying with wooden spools at the foot of the red plum tree, rolling them back and forth with his bill. "Anna does not puff out luminous emerald feathers like Anna's hummingbird, but she is just as charming!" the songbird muses.

This is why, when Odin hears that Anna's world-famous apple strudel – the one with a sprinkle of cinnamon and walnuts – has disappeared, he dashes to the garden to offer consolation. He is furious at the villain who had the audacity to steal the strudel right under her nose. And to make matters worse, Anna's old sewing thimble is missing, as well.

"Rats! Well, how about that?" he meows, wiggling his thick whiskers.

4

In spite of everything, Anna is not too distressed as to how this unfortunate petty thievery happened. There is plenty of work to be done, so she stands over a delicate cotton fabric laid on the large kitchen table, humming a melody. She is about to make magic with her white tailor's chalk as she begins to mark smooth, elaborate lines on it. Her concentration is tangible, and Odin studies her every movement. What's more, he is bedazzled by this mysterious glow, so like a misty moon halo, above her pretty head.

"Goodness me! Can anyone else see it, or is it just a figment of my imagination?" he mumbles to himself.

After hand-basting long, loose stitches, Anna walks to the ancient sewing machine known as the Singer, a tireless companion that has sustained her throughout the years. And then Odin hears the familiar sound of her foot dancing on the machine's pedal while the needle makes precise, almost invisible, stitches.

Lulled by the soothing noise of sewing, Odin gets comfortable on the cool stone sill and waits patiently.

In the meantime, the brown-eyed dog called Ollie wakes up from his nap. He is the world champion of siestas, considering that snoozing is one of his life's ambitions. Needless to say, the peace and quiet in the garden is now ancient history. Ignoring his pride, Ollie races to the windowsill, sits upright and begins to beg for a bite with his paws. His wish will be granted because that is what Anna does: she grants wishes.

"I am famished. Feed me!" he woofs, wagging his tail.

Odin, also described as "the one of the fussy feline world", does not really mind canines. Dogs have never chased or bothered him since they are all terrified of his claws. All the same, he shows very little regard for Ollie. In his opinion, he is unpredictable and tediously dull, and he smells ghastly. It is true that these days he appears to be as clean as a whistle, and that itself is a surprising turn of events.

Besides the nagging appetite, Ollie's gut instincts tell him that something is not right. Anna is very quiet, and Odin seems edgy. And then it hits him. "Oh no! A theft in my neck of the woods: that is a despicable act."

The garden's gate opens screeching, and a young boy from the neighbourhood walks in. His name is Maxie, but friends have nicknamed him Merlin like the fierce falcon, and because of his considerable expertise in ornithology. He is also a serious collector of comic books and the proud owner of a dreamcatcher. He greets Anna merrily and sits at the top of the stone steps, holding a book in one hand and an ice-cream cone in the other. "My freshly baked apple strudel has vanished into thin air!" Anna blurts out on impulse.

"Good grief! The one with walnuts and no raisins, for my sake? We cannot lose the great apple-walnut," Maxie yells, his face turning as red as a beet. On top of everything, he nearly jumps out of his skin when Ollie's muzzle suddenly slams into his clenched hand. A split second later, and the ice-cream cone is gone, too. There is no regret in the dog's eyes because he knows well Maxie's forgiving nature.

"That mutt has a screw loose! He is a menace and a troublemaker," the cat sighs, full of contempt.

Maxie has been drawn to this garden for as long as he can remember. The reason is quite simple. It is the only place where he can read in peace. He itches for the excitement of setting foot in brave new worlds and building his own castles in the air. And he is equally fascinated by the extraordinary drawings and the speech bubbles overflowing with whams and bams.

The fact of the matter is that Maxie has always had artistic aspirations. Just recently, while browsing through the tale of a whimsical wild goat, he sketched some seriously beautiful drawings. Luckily for him, he has never been discouraged from pursuing a career as a painter.

The following is a brief account of the goat named Kid and her breathless rock-climbing journeys along mountain snow lines and above forests.

To begin with, Kid prides herself on being the best rock climber in the herd. A true daredevil. But, every now and then, she loses her way while leaping from one jaw-dropping rocky ledge to another – foraging for silky moss and, the old favourite, licking salty stones. She is absent-minded and often wanders off aimlessly here and there. All the same, she is very cautious not to fall prey to eagles, since she has had too many nightmares haunted by their hooked beaks.

What is more, Kid adores humming melodies, and she has an exquisite ear for music. When descending the steep slopes, she fantasizes about minstrels playing magical ballads.

14

Here is a true portrait of Kid's imaginary minstrels: there is a lanky white-haired giant with a superb guitar, its sound soaring high above the winds; a handsome poet with a lion's mane, his magnificent voice lending grace to a march that narrates of faraway places; and a mysterious maestro who calls the tune.

Still reluctant to end her dream, Kid wisely resolves to find the herd before nightfall. "I can move mountains with my imagination, but I am too young to go out into the world alone."

16

After that, there is the time when Kid decides to conquer the highest mountaintop and see shooting stars up close. She wishes for not a care in the world. Bear in mind that she is under great strain, as she keeps losing things: the blue ribbon tied to one of the horns, a bucket of creamy cheese, a precious book of lullabies, and just recently – sigh – her cherished uncle Billy.

When Kid reaches the snow-capped peak, she closes her eyes and ruminates for a short while to dull the sorrow. Armed with her vivid imagination, she wishes for the brightest star to shatter into sparkling bits. And it does! Caught off guard, thunderstruck, Kid tumbles down the mountain and lands on rugged ground. Much to her surprise, she stands face to face with piles of books just lying around. What's more, she can hear hushed whispers saying: Come this way please, let us tell you about the great philosophers, so you can figure out who you are and why you are here?

Kid is flabbergasted. "What planet have I fallen onto?"

At the same time something unexpected captures her attention.There is an apple strudel lying on the ground, filling the air with sweet fragrance, and a splendid dreamcatcher swaying from a withered branch. "All right, kiddo, it's time to leave this dream," she says to herself, feeling a little uneasy.

Maxie shuts the book hastily. This is one of the most bizarre things that has ever happened to him.

"What on earth is Anna's apple strudel doing in my book? How did it get into Kid's dream?" he cries out, feeling a twinge of guilt.

Meanwhile, Anna has made a frittata of eggs and wild asparagus. No dessert, for obvious reasons, even if there is never a shortage of home-made chocolate chip cookies in her kitchen.

She asks Maxie to join her, and he accepts readily. Anna knows that he is enthusiastic about her home cooking – first and foremost, the cakes. She has many times enjoyed the stories of his travels, and besides, he might offer some insight into this awful incident.

20

Maxie is determined to astonish Anna with his new adventure. He takes over the narrator's role seriously because it fits him like a glove.

"It was a warm summer morning soon after daybreak. I was walking along a trail, lost in deep contemplation. All of a sudden, the silence was broken by a crackle-crunch noise. Far too loud to be a bird or a lizard, I thought. And then the noise emerged from a thorny hedgerow on its four legs.

A large badger crossed the trail in no rush. Thankfully it ignored me, and disappeared on the opposite side – towards the seashore, apparently, as I could smell the salty air. I was too stunned to be alarmed but kept walking. Well, perhaps a little faster!"

"Shortly afterwards I stumbled upon this extraordinary place – a tiny swamp in the middle of nowhere. A haven of tranquillity for its many tenants and visitors. Egrets, dressed in white, lined up on dry heaps of grass, looking like a welcome committee. A kingfisher swooped down from a perch like a flash of bright colour, while other winged beauties glided gracefully over the water.

Half-hidden in the tall grass, I sat spellbound, admiring their elegant flight."

24

"I had lost all track of time, but my belly started to rumble pretty loudly, and my legs felt like jelly. I dived into my backpack and found a heavenly mortadella-ham sandwich, a cream doughnut and a bottle of peach iced tea. Somebody must have read my mind.

Was it aunt Follia? My favourite aunt is worthy of her nickname, which means folly in Italian, no doubt. She gave me a fantastic dreamcatcher from the Great Lakes, and said it was once owned by an old shaman. I don't know if it's true, but it doesn't matter. What matters is that, according to legend, dreamcatchers can catch bad dreams in their webs and let the good ones flow over the sleeper.

I still remember the first time, when I waited the whole day for the night to fall, anxious to plunge into the land of dreams. Dazed but overjoyed! Since then, I have always carried it with me, as it is my most precious possession."

"I might have dozed off clutching the dreamcatcher, and I dreamed of a sleepy village standing atop a towering hill on an island. Drenched in sunlight. The name on the signpost read Head of the Island.

I was marching along a narrow road, escorted by olive groves and fig trees, and the persistent scent of lavender. My great-grandmother's old cupboards were filled with cotton nets of dried lavender. The sweet memories of her made me grin from ear to ear."

28

"On top of that, I had the distinct feeling of being watched. Sure enough, there was a curious donkey eyeing me with suspicion and distrust. His stare said it all – I warn you boy, I am prepared not to like you!

The donkey had a bump between his eyes, so there and then, I named him Don Bumpy. Ha ha! Most likely he once fantasized about being a feisty bull and charged some unfortunate olive tree.

My friend Roxie would be thrilled by this encounter, as she thinks donkeys are fascinating creatures. For the record, Roxie is a tree whisperer, but that's another story."

"Then, out of the blue, I spotted a Griffon vulture lying motionless on the ground, hurt but alive. Without hesitation I carried the bird to the sanctuary, followed by the donkey's approving look.

On the roof of the shelter there were other ailing vultures, stretching their wings as soon as the sun peeked out from behind the clouds. I couldn't take my eyes off them for a long time: what a sight! And then I woke up under a splendid sky at sundown while the sea was ruffled by gusts of the bora wind."

Anna sits in silence, marvelling at Maxie's flair for storytelling.

There is a sharp knock at the front door. It must be Anna's weird neighbour, Silly Maggie, who drops in uninvited at all hours. She walks around in her bathrobe – which, by the way, can barely conceal her chubby figure – and her hair is usually tangled around ugly curlers. Without fail, she asks to borrow things such as pincushions, pots and pans and whatnot. Clearly, her visits are an excuse to nose around and examine Anna's food for flaws and faults with her bulging eyes. She has heard about the theft, and is more than ready to gossip about it.

"The pompous bore!" mutters Maxie under his breath.

34

Ollie detests being ignored. He barks wildly and jumps back and forth over the large hortensia, making its pink blossoms sway from side to side, desperate to get Anna's attention. At last, she comes to the window with a jar of delectable cookies just for him, and Ollie is thrilled to bits.

36

All along, Fin, the watchful finch, has been observing the ways of the world from his red plum tree. The garden is too crowded and noisy for his liking. What is this horrible hullabaloo about anyway?

Fin has a solitary, placid temperament very unlike the other finches. Therefore, he decides to collect the seeds and cherries that Anna puts on the windowsill for him alone at a later time. If they knew what Fin had seen, the puzzle would be solved already.

"Attention, please! Has anyone noticed a boy tucking something away in his backpack in a great hurry? I am a little bird with a big secret. Fancy that!" he trills with sheer satisfaction, fluffing his raspberry-coloured feathers. But that is not Fin's only secret. Stashed away in his nest, he hides Anna's glossy thimble. Wicked!

38

When all is said and done, it is business as usual in the garden, and they all carry on with their lives. Odin savours a bowl of milk, while Ollie gets ready for another long afternoon nap. Silly Maggie goes home to get dressed and fix her hair for a change.

Maxie is spotted heading into deep woodland. "To see hawks," he says – gulping down the last bite of Anna's swirling apple strudel. He could not resist the temptation, but vows to make amends for this vile behaviour. After all, she is the kindest and most compassionate soul he has ever met.

Anna plans to bake another apple strudel, unaware that she is in for a big surprise upon Maxie's return.

Perched high in the red plum tree, the finch chirps, "What a lot of fuss about nothing!"

40

Acknowledgements

For their advice and assistance, thanks to: Lilia, my illustrator, with much admiration, and Andy for the constructive editing. Special thanks to Dorian for providing the inspiration.